IF FOUN 

MW00883136

Greater Than a Tourist Book Series
Reviews from Readers

I think the series is wonderful and beneficial for tourists to get information before visiting the city.

-Seckin Zumbul, Izmir Turkey

I am a world traveler who has read many trip guides but this one really made a difference for me. I would call it a heartfelt creation of a local guide expert instead of just a guide.

-Susy, Isla Holbox, Mexico

New to the area like me, this is a must have!

-Joe, Bloomington, USA

This is a good series that gets down to it when looking for things to do at your destination without having to read a novel for just a few ideas.

-Rachel, Monterey, USA

Good information to have to plan my trip to this destination.

-Pennie Farrell, Mexico

Great ideas for a port day.

-Mary Martin USA

Aptly titled, you won't just be a tourist after reading this book. You'll be greater than a tourist!

-Alan Warner, Grand Rapids, USA

Even though I only have three days to spend in San Miguel in an upcoming visit, I will use the author's suggestions to guide some of my time there. An easy read - with chapters named to guide me in directions I want to go.

-Robert Catapano, USA

Great insights from a local perspective! Useful information and a very good value!

-Sarah, USA

This series provides an in-depth experience through the eyes of a local. Reading these series will help you to travel the city in with confidence and it'll make your journey a unique one.

-Andrew Teoh, Ipoh, Malaysia

GREATER THAN A TOURIST- CAIRO EGYPT

50 Travel Tips from a Local

Gihan Amin

Greater Than a Tourist- Cairo Egypt Copyright © 2018 by CZYK Publishing LLC. All Rights Reserved.

All rights reserved. No part of this book may be reproduced in any form or by any electronic or mechanical means including information storage and retrieval systems, without permission in writing from the author. The only exception is by a reviewer, who may quote short excerpts in a review.

The statements in this book are of the authors and may not be the views of CZYK Publishing or Greater Than a Tourist.

Cover Template Creator: Lisa Rusczyk Ed. D. using Canva.
Cover Creator: Lisa Rusczyk Ed. D.
Image: https://pixabay.com/en/pyramids-egypt-cairo-giza-tourism-2499780/
https://pixabay.com/en/cairo-home-city-building-roofs-768281/

Edited by: Timothy Dobos

CZYK Publishing Since 2011.

Greater Than a Tourist
Visit our website at www.GreaterThanaTourist.com

Lock Haven, PA
All rights reserved.
ISBN: 9781790430048

>TOURIST

50 TRAVEL TIPS FROM A LOCAL

BOOK DESCRIPTION

Are you excited about planning your next trip?

Do you want to try something new?

Would you like some guidance from a local?

If you answered yes to any of these questions, then this Greater Than a Tourist book is for you.

Greater Than a Tourist –Cairo Egypt by Gihan Amin offers the inside scoop on the city of Cairo. Most travel books tell you how to travel like a tourist. Although there is nothing wrong with that, as part of the Greater Than a Tourist series, this book will give you travel tips from someone who has lived at your next travel destination.

In these pages, you will discover advice that will help you throughout your stay. This book will not tell you exact addresses or store hours but instead will give you excitement and knowledge from a local that you may not find in other smaller print travel books.

Travel like a local. Slow down, stay in one place, and get to know the people and the culture. By the time you finish this book, you will be eager and prepared to travel to your next destination.

TABLE OF CONTENTS

BOOK DESCRIPTION
TABLE OF CONTENTS
DEDICATION
ABOUT THE AUTHOR
HOW TO USE THIS BOOK
FROM THE PUBLISHER
OUR STORY
WELCOME TO
> TOURIST
INTRODUCTION
1. Beware Of The Daily Weather
2. Carry A Bottle Of Water Wherever You Go
3. Best Means Of Transportation In Cairo
4. Where To Stay
5. Enjoy The Typical Egyptian Breakfast
6. Ride A Caretta
7. Eat A Meal At Zainab Khatoun Café In Old Cairo
8. Attend A Festival At Darb 1718
9. Ride A Camel And Visit The Pyramids
10. Drink Sobia And Assab
11. Where To Shop For Authentic Souvenirs
12. Phrases To Learn
13. Join Cairo Runners For A Morning Run
14. Visit Cairo Tower

15. Visit Prince Mohamed Ali's Palace
16. Eat Assab
17. Enjoy A Fancy Breakfast at Al Korba Street Between The Old Buildings
18. Escape Like A Cairo Resident
19. Meals To Try
20. Attend One Of Al Sawy Cultural Wheel Events
21. Book A Cruise In The Nile
22. Watch a Football Game Like a Local
23. Sing Your Soul Away On Christmas Eve In One Of Cairo's Celebrations
24. Catch Sunset At Al Mokattam
25. Treat Yourself With A Konafa Plate
26. Visit The Underground Church
27. Take A Walk In Al Moez Street At Night
28. Eat Hummus Al Sham While Listening To Oum Kalthoum At The Shores Of The Nile
29. Take A Walk Downtown
30. Where To Shop For Clothes
31. Watch A Tanoura Dance At Wekalet El Ghoury
32. Catch The Spring Festival At Al Orman Gardens
33. Walk And Explore The Island of Maadi
34. Visit Ibn Tulun Mosque
35. Visit Al Azhar
36. Newly-Opened Museums You Need to Visit
37. Palaces You Must Visit

38. Eat Like A Local During Easter
39. Walk In Cairo's Most Beautiful Parks
40. Be One Of Cairo's Animal Enthusiasts
41. Spend A Fancy Night At Cairo Opera House
42. Nola Yourself
43. Dance And Watch Them Dance
44. Take A Nile Tour In A Felucca
45. Go Sandboarding
46. Explore Al Moez Li Din Allah Street
47. Go Clubbing Like A Local
48. Pictures To Take
49. Visit Coptic Cairo
50. Do The One Day Trips From Cairo
50 THINGS TO KNOW ABOUT PACKING LIGHT FOR TRAVEL
Packing and Planning Tips
Travel Questions
Travel Bucket List
NOTES

DEDICATION

This book is dedicated to my beautiful country and its extraordinarily loveable people.

ABOUT THE AUTHOR

Gihan Amin is an Egyptian who lives in Cairo, Egypt, where she currently studies Architectural engineering. She loves dogs, travelling, reading and writing. She lived in Egypt since she was a child, and wandering in the streets of Cairo is her favorite hobby. Between almost 99 million residents that live in Cairo, she feels a deeper connection between her and the streets of her city.

The streets of Cairo represent a home for her. Between the walls of history and the busy modern lifestyle, Cairo granted her a feeling of warmth and serenity. What she likes about her city is that it witnessed the victories, losses, and wars of several dynasties throughout the years. Cairo accommodates numerous mosques, churches, and palaces that left question marks for her and triggered her mind to look for answers and to know more about her home.

The modernity of Cairo never set traditions, lame or mocked. Even though Cairo is a modern city, in which you can enjoy everything, from night clubs to mosques and churches, it has never set its traditions aside. Being a resident of the city of Cairo, you will know how much love its people hold for each other. Cairo's residents will help you whenever you need help, will love you for no reason, will accept you, just the way you are, and will grant you with the warmth of a home and family.

HOW TO USE THIS BOOK

The Greater Than a Tourist book series was written by someone who has lived in an area for over three months. The goal of this book is to help travelers either dream or experience different locations by providing opinions from a local. The author has made suggestions based on their own experiences. Please do your own research before traveling to the area in case the suggested places are unavailable.

Travel Advisories: As a first step in planning any trip abroad, check the Travel Advisories for your intended destination.
https://travel.state.gov/content/travel/en/traveladvisories/traveladvisories.html

FROM THE PUBLISHER

Traveling can be one of the most important parts of a person's life. The anticipation and memories that you have are some of the best. As a publisher of the Greater Than a Tourist book series, as well as the popular 50 Things to Know book series, we strive to help you learn about new places, spark your imagination, and inspire you. Wherever you are and whatever you do I wish you safe, fun, and inspiring travel.

Lisa Rusczyk Ed. D.
CZYK Publishing

OUR STORY

Traveling is a passion of the "Greater than a Tourist" series creator. Lisa studied abroad in college, and for their honeymoon Lisa and her husband toured Europe. During her travels to Malta, an older man tried to give her some advice based on his own experience living on the island since he was a young boy. She was not sure if she should talk to the stranger but was interested in his advice. When traveling to some places she was wary to talk to locals because she was afraid that they weren't being genuine. Through her travels, Lisa learned how much locals had to share with tourists. Lisa created the "Greater Than a Tourist" book series to help connect people with locals. A topic that locals are very passionate about sharing.

WELCOME TO
> TOURIST

INTRODUCTION

The best way to go about a country or city, in my opinion, is to know its residents' traditions, culture and interests. For this reason, this books grants you a full local experience. In this book, you will be able to know everything that Cairo residents do to have fun, their traditions, and culture. Another great way of discovering Cairo is to have its map with you. Like this, you will be able to get back to your hotel if you ever get lost.

1. BEWARE OF THE DAILY WEATHER

Even though Egypt is known for its beautiful weather, you have to beware of its daily weather changes. The first phase Cairo's weather endures is the chilly morning phase. This phase starts from dawn, approximately at 4 AM, and lasts till 7 AM. During these three hours, Cairo's weather tends to be chilly, accompanied with cold breeze.

The second weather phase in Cairo starts roughly at 8 AM and lasts almost until 5 PM. During this time of the day, the weather is usually hot and enjoyable, which allows you to literally do anything you want, from shopping to sightseeing.

The last phase of Cairo's daily weather tends to be similar to that of the first phase. It starts from 6 PM and lasts till the dawn of the next day. This phase is characterized with fresh air and cool breezes, which allows you to go jogging, shopping or simply hang around the Nile and enjoy a felucca tour.

2. CARRY A BOTTLE OF WATER WHEREVER YOU GO

Cairo's weather tends to be very hot during the middle of the day, so it is a must to always carry a bottle of water with you wherever you go. Take it from a local, buy your bottle of water from a kiosk or a super market that is not located near any historical monuments because supermarkets located near historical monuments tend to be 5 LE (Egyptian pounds) more expensive, if not more.

The Nile city, of course, has free drinkable water, so make sure to ask the room service at the hotel that you're staying in if the faucet water is drinkable. Any normal house in Cairo drinks from the faucet water, using a water filter of course, for more safety.

3. BEST MEANS OF TRANSPORTATION IN CAIRO

Transportation around Cairo can be frustrating. However, if you know the best means of transportation, you will not face any problems. Your best bet is Uber or Careem, so you have to make sure that you download both mobile apps to ensure that you have safe and fast rides around Cairo.

Usually, the problem with transportation in Cairo is the traffic. So, to avoid this, you can book a Careem motorcycle, or a Nile taxi that assures a fast, safe, and enjoyable trip.

Lastly, the best means of transportation around Cairo, and I might also say cheapest, is Metro. Taking the Metro allows you to save time and money because its ticket is affordable and, need I not say, it's much faster than any other means of transportation in Cairo.

4. WHERE TO STAY

Cairo is full of hotels. However, as a local, I would recommend that you take a deeper look at the hotels while choosing. The best hotels around Cairo are either the ones with a good view of historical monuments, such as the hotels located near the pyramids, or the hotels located around new Cairo and Tagamo'. Both categories have unique advantages, as the hotels located in New Cairo are closer to the best shopping malls in Cairo , while hotels located near old Cairo and pyramids grant you with a beautiful selection of historical buildings to visit.

5. ENJOY THE TYPICAL EGYPTIAN BREAKFAST

Foul and Falafel are the typical Egyptian breakfast. As a local, I prefer this meal either from a Foul Car or from one of Al Korba street food outlets. Foul is basically beans, however, what makes it special is the Egyptian flavors added. The best Foul sandwiches to eat in Cairo are the Alexandrian Foul and Baladi (local) Foul.

6. RIDE A CARETTA

A Caretta tour is literally one of the most enjoyable things to do in Cairo, especially one around the Nile. A Caretta is a small car, driven by strong horses and a driver that leads them. If you are lucky, you will find a Caretta around the shores of the Nile because these cars are not numerous.

Try to take this Caretta ride with a Cairo resident. To do so, you can simply initiate that you need company during your stay in Cairo on Cairo Confessions Facebook page , and you will surely find loads of people who would gratefully show you around Cairo and help you find a Caretta.

7. EAT A MEAL AT ZAINAB KHATOUN CAFÉ IN OLD CAIRO

Zeinab Khatoun is a café located in Al Moez street, between the old historical buildings. This street is one where you can enjoy Cairo's history, its festivals, souvenir shops, and Tanoura shops. Hunt for this Café in the seasons of festivals, Tanoura shows and local singers in Al Moez street festivals, between the walls of history, and eat local Egyptian food, such as Fattah or Mahshy (Vine Leaves).

8. ATTEND A FESTIVAL AT DARB 1718

Darb 1718 is your ultimate escape if you are looking for a cultural or artistic shows. This place, located in Old Cairo, accommodates the finest contemporary art shows in Cairo as well as a variety of activities and workshops. The workshops include writing, recycling, yoga, mosaic, photography, and many more choices. Also, the activities you can enjoy there vary from mawaweel festivals to street art.

9. RIDE A CAMEL AND VISIT THE PYRAMIDS

Of course, the first thing that comes to your mind when you hear the word "Cairo" is the pyramids, and no one can blame you, the pyramids are mind-blowing! Even locals visit the pyramids at least once a year. As a local, my only advice is to ride a camel and take as many pictures as your camera's memory card can afford.

The camels are what makes this visit authentic. Ancient Egyptians used to use camels as their means of transportation and this is exactly why you should never miss getting on the back of a camel. Also, be careful and treat the camels delicately, as these animals are very sensitive. Another thing that you can try is riding a horse there. Alright to be honest, near the pyramids, you will find multiple exciting things to do, but for me, I find it really enjoyable to blend in with the locals, tourists, and animals.

10. DRINK SOBIA AND ASSAB

Assab and Sobia are the two main Local's drink in Cairo. Assab is the sugar cane fruit drink. This drink can only be found in Egypt. On the other hand, Sobia is a coconut flavored drink. Both drinks cannot be found in super markets or kiosks, you can only find them in cafés, natural juice markets, and, sometimes, in restaurants.

"Cairo is an exploding modern metropolis which nevertheless preserves within its heart the finest medieval city in the world..."

— Michael Haag

11. WHERE TO SHOP FOR AUTHENTIC SOUVENIRS

Al Moez street and Old Cairo, also known as Coptic Cairo, are the best places for authentic souvenirs. The real souvenirs that would remind you of Cairo are small pyramids, Nefertiti and Abou El-Houl statues and a Tarboush (an old fashioned red hat). These souvenirs are not expensive, so make sure to buy them from Khan Al Khalili and Coptic Cairo. Also, if you are in a hurry and cannot go to Khan Al Khalili, you can simply go to City Stars located in Nasr City and quickly pass by the Khan Al Khalili Section to buy a souvenir, but it will be expensive.

12. PHRASES TO LEARN

Arabic is a fun language to learn--that's until you hear the Egyptian language and it becomes your favorite. Egyptians invented slang that composed a language of its own. Here are a few phrases you need to learn before you initiate a conversation with a local:

Alf shokr: This one stands for thank you, or a million thanks to be more specific.

Ahbes be shay: This phrase indicates the act of drinking tea after eating a heavy meal. It is usually used between locals anywhere and everywhere around Cairo, even in fancy restaurants.

Eshta: Peace, as simple as that. Eshta for Cairo residents means peace, however, its real meaning is cream. This word is commonly used even by kids, so be ready to hear it at least twice per day.

13. JOIN CAIRO RUNNERS FOR A MORNING RUN

The residents of Cairo are very energetic, and one morning run with them will benefit you, for sure. Cairo Runners is an organization that has a page on Facebook. Look it up and stay tuned for one of their morning runs. It will have you waiting for more events. Cairo Runners for me is the best negative energy extractor, where I just go run, meet new people, socialize, enjoy the giveaways, and refresh my energy.

14. VISIT CAIRO TOWER

The highest spot in Cairo will definitely be waiting for you. There, take your time taking pictures and enjoying the view. The most important thing when you're up there is to take care while taking pictures because your phone might slip and fall. Apart from that, the place and view are spectacular and cannot be missed.

Watch sunset there. If you are lucky enough, you will be able to catch sunset from such high of a point. What makes this special is the amount of couples and families you will meet there. You will be surprised by how much love Cairo residents hold in their hearts when you see families going there to have a day together.

15. VISIT PRINCE MOHAMED ALI'S PALACE

Prince Mohamed Ali's palace, located on Rhoda Island

in the Nile, is a palace that you cannot miss during your stay in Cairo. This palace is composed of six buildings, each representing a different dynasty. The Mamelukes, Ottoman, and Rocco left their mark on the architecture of Cairo in this palace.

A collection of paintings, books, and collections that

belong to the royals are kept there. If you are looking for a

royal experience, go there. Another plus for this place is the parks and gardens, where you will find rare plants.

16. EAT ASSAB

If you're looking for a delicious Egyptian fruit to sip on in a hot summer day, then it is definitely Assab (sugar canes). To eat Assab, you need to follow a certain technique. In order to learn this technique, you need to watch someone eat it. My advice to you is to buy only one sugar cane for yourself and sit with a local to learn how to eat it and enjoy its sugary flavor.

17. ENJOY A FANCY BREAKFAST AT AL KORBA STREET BETWEEN THE OLD BUILDINGS

Al Korba neighborhood is one of the oldest neighborhoods in Cairo, where old buildings stand proudly. This neighborhood is one of the best places to enjoy a royal breakfast. Café Supreme, TBS, and Paul are my three favorite food outlets at Al Korba neighborhood. Even though these three restaurants are exceptional, I would always recommend to take a tour in the neighborhood to try for yourself and decide which restaurant grants you with both, a good view of the old buildings and delicious food.

18. ESCAPE LIKE A CAIRO RESIDENT

What most tourist don't know, is that Cairo is FULL of activities. Escape rooms, Air zone, Paint Ball and Battle field are, in my opinion, the most entertaining games to play if you have a big group and want to have some fun. If you are an energetic group, then head to New Cairo, Al Tagamo' specifically, where you will find most of these activities. First of all, the escape rooms, are not only adrenaline stimulators, but also mind activating, as you have to solve equations, one after another, in order to be able to get free. Also, if you just want to play and have fun, then paint ball and battle field will grant you this experience. The most important thing in these games is to have a fun spirit and an energetic group that is up for a good fight. Lastly, if you simply want to have fun, no teams, no winners or fights, then Air Zone Trampolines are your best resort. You can go and unleash your inner child.

19. MEALS TO TRY

Cairo is known for its mouthwatering meals; however, some meals are a must. You can start with eating a Molokheya with rice and chicken meal; this is a typical Egyptian meal that you can find in Oriental food restaurants. Also, vine leaves and Hamam are one of the most delicious meals that will have you coming back for more and more. And lastly, you have to try all types of Mahshy and eat a plate of Koshary.

20. ATTEND ONE OF AL SAWY CULTURAL WHEEL EVENTS

If you're naturally an art lover, then Al Sawy Cultural Wheel is your place. This place hosts the finest musical events, as well as cultural seminars, puppet theatre, workshops, and courses. Some seminars address social problems, while others discuss global issues. In this place, you will definitely find a campaign or seminar that interests you.

Try to attend one campaign of your interest, if you're someone looking for an event with a cause to attend. If not, you will find plenty of musical events held there on weekly basis, a variety of music bands, specialized in their own musical genres. Mark your calendar for one the best nights you will spend in Cairo.

"Cairo is one of the greatest storehouses of human achievement on earth, ranging from the pharaonic through the Christian and Islamic periods to the Belle Epoque."

— *Michael Haag*.

21. BOOK A CRUISE IN THE NILE

If you are a nature enthusiast, then this cruise will bring you joy and peace. The Nile river is very long and overlooks beautiful terrains of fruits and vegetables. Also, if you are more of a person who enjoys buildings, you will have a good view of the Pyramids and the high buildings of Cairo. Moreover, it is a must to watch the sunset on a boat in the Nile. This sight is one that cannot be missed when in Cairo. And if you have time, take a Nile cruise for three days, from Cairo to Aswan and back from Aswan to Cairo, enjoying the history of Aswan and its temples, the beauty of the Nile, and its generosity.

22. WATCH A FOOTBALL GAME LIKE A LOCAL

In Cairo, football matches are a sacred passion. If you're lucky, you would be able to watch a match for Al Ahly club vs Al Zamalek club, in a local coffee shop. These matches gather crowds and crowds to any coffee shop. Also, if your options do not include the aforementioned teams, Egyptians watch Premier League, La Liga and Champion's League as well. Attend a match of your own choice.

This experience reaches its best combination if you choose a "ahwa balady" which stands for a local coffee shop. Of course, fancy coffee shops are also fine; however, the football spirit is very vibrant at the local coffee shops.

23. SING YOUR SOUL AWAY ON CHRISTMAS EVE IN ONE OF CAIRO'S CELEBRATIONS

Cairo is one of the cities that celebrates Christmas Eve in a very unique way. Every hotel in Cairo holds Christmas carols. After the choir is over, mind blowing music and DJs start their mission. Christmas carols in Cairo have a spectacular taste, as every attendant wears nice colorful clothes, beautiful dresses for the ladies and sophisticated suits for gentlemen. Attend one of those events at one of the Fairmont hotels or Dusit Thani. You will be amazed by the spirit and music.

24. CATCH SUNSET AT AL MOKATTAM

Sunset at the highest spot in Cairo is a breathtaking sight to see. Honestly, the view from up there, at Al Mokattam, is spectacular to the point that it has locals from different parts of

Cairo drive more than two hours to catch a forty-five-minute scene.

25. TREAT YOURSELF WITH A KONAFA PLATE

Konafa is the typical Egyptian desert. Locals eat Konafa on daily basis; however, I would always recommend to eat small portions, if you are going to eat it every day. The best places to try Konafa are: Konafa Ala El Fahm and Coper Melt Deserts. The former is a Konafa restaurant at Al Rehab city that makes grilled Konafa. The latter is not a restaurant. However, its Konafa is unbelievably tasty.

26. VISIT THE UNDERGROUND CHURCH

The underground church is one of Cairo's hidden gems. This church is located at Hay Al Zabaleen. Even though this church is not located near the rest of the historical monuments, it is one worth seeing. This church lays underground, the shrines are underground, the statues are underground and even the seats are underground. Look it up on the internet and catch this beauty before it's famous and busy.

27. TAKE A WALK IN AL MOEZ STREET AT NIGHT

Al Moez Street is known for being the street that accommodates most of Cairo's historical buildings; however, it is so much more than that. Al Moez Street is the heart of old Cairo. Between the streets of this district, you will be amazed by how Cairo has changed. Take your time examining the buildings around you, while sipping on a cup of tea, and notice how history is written all over the old buildings.

28. EAT HUMMUS AL SHAM WHILE LISTENING TO OUM KALTHOUM AT THE SHORES OF THE NILE

If you're travelling with your wife, fiancée or girlfriend, take her to the Nile and eat Hummus Al Sham. This is the typical place for couples to have a modest outing in Cairo, where you can enjoy modesty, beauty, and good music.

29. TAKE A WALK DOWNTOWN

Downtown Cairo is one of the most energetic spots in town. I, personally, go there whenever I feel like it, to enjoy its various shops and restaurants. You can literally do anything in Downtown Cairo. You can go shopping, sightseeing--and even go to the movies or attend a live theatre show.

Downtown is your escape whenever you feel like walking while eating a scoop of ice cream, watching people come and go while sipping on a cup of coffee, or even shopping with your family. There, you will find Groppi, the famous bakery, Simonds, one of the best morning coffee stops in Cairo, and even the one and only Greek Club where you can enjoy their delicious French fries along with their Greek salad, good music and mesmerizing view of the streets of Cairo from the open area.

30. WHERE TO SHOP FOR CLOTHES

If you want to shop for clothes, head to Cairo's busiest malls, such as Mall of Arabia or Mall of Egypt. These two malls are located in the 6th of October city, and you can even enjoy an adventurous experience at Ski Egypt at Mall of Egypt. Ski Egypt is an indoor ski experience where you can enjoy the freezing weather accompanied with snow and multiple activities.

City Stars Mall, Cairo Festival City Mall and Downtown Mall, are located in Nasr City and New Cairo respectively. In these malls, you can find both local and international brands. Take a look at the rising local Egyptian brands. You won't regret it.

"One of my favourite things to think about is, if you could be invisible and go back in time, where would you go? I've always said ancient Egypt. I would love to see them building the pyramids, and I've always had a real fascination with medieval time and monarchy in medieval times."

- Elizabeth Debicki

31. WATCH A TANOURA DANCE AT WEKALET EL GHOURY

Tanoura shows are Egyptian shows in which a strong man wears a Tanoura (long colorful skirt) and twirls around with mizmar (a musical instrument) rhythms. This show is one that brings in indescribable amounts of joy and happiness. Go watch one of these shows at Wekalet El Ghoury, drink a cup of tea, and blend in with Cairo's residents. Also, you can look up Wekalet El Ghoury's location on your GPS to ensure you arrive at the right place.

32. CATCH THE SPRING FESTIVAL AT AL ORMAN GARDENS

Unfortunately, tourists do not know that Cairo is full of gardens, and one the most beautiful gardens of Cairo is Al Orman garden. This garden is colorful, full of flowers and trees. And, this particular garden can be compared to a green carpet. However, I would always recommend to visit it during the spring festivals. During spring festivals, this garden is full of flower shops that come and display their most colorful flowers. As a local, I attend this festival every year to enjoy the spring spirit, socialize, and take good pictures.

33. WALK AND EXPLORE THE ISLAND OF MAADI

El Maadi is a beautiful district that lays on one side of the Nile, and, being granted with Maadi Island, makes it even more spectacular. Maadi Island surrounds a bifurcation of the Nile and envelops it with its green carpets. This garden has it all. Whenever you feel like chilling in fresh air, natural scenes and good food, then it is the perfect choice.

Maadi District is known for its restaurants. If you choose to go to Maadi Island, take a tour in Street 9 in Maadi and grab something to eat before or after your visit to the island.

34. VISIT IBN TULUN MOSQUE

Ibn Tulun Mosque is the oldest surviving mosque in the city of Cairo. What makes this mosque very unique is that it has managed to keep its shape, form, design and decoration throughout the years. The mosque was one of the first mosques to have a ziyada (extra land surrounding the praying area). Also, take your time while examining its malweya minaret, as it is one of the very few malweya minarets in Cairo, and the window grills of this authentic mosque, as it contains 128 window grills, each having a unique design.

35. VISIT AL AZHAR

Al Azhar district, literally, gives you all you'll ever wish for, in one place. Not only a range of historical monuments, beautiful mosques, and distinguished palaces lay there, but also, Al Azhar is considered as one of the most important fabric outlets in Egypt. In Al Azhar, you will find any type of fabric you want, you name it, from linen and cotton to carpet fabrics. The best thing about Al Azhar is the low prices and good quality. Take a tour before you buy anything, ask in more than one shop, and make your decision for the best quality and affordable price. And, as a rule, do not buy from the first shop you enter.

Al Azhar district is also close to Bab Al Fotouh, Al Hussein and Al Moez Street. Take a tour in all these streets; they are indescribable. The mosques and palaces there are not normal, not a single street is free of monuments, so make this tour a fruitful one.

36. NEWLY-OPENED MUSEUMS YOU NEED TO VISIT

Recently, multiple museum projects have been launched all around Cairo. The National Museum of Egyptian Civilisation is one of these museums. This museum is an outstanding one as its design is unique as well as its valuable statues. The design of this museum is green, which allows natural light to warm up the museum halls. The purpose of this museum is to show the Egyptian civilisation, so do not miss it. Another museum that is yet to open in mid-2018 is the Grand Egyptian museum. This museum is still under construction; however, it is expected to be the largest archeological museum in the world.

37. PALACES YOU MUST VISIT

Old Cairo basically consists of the finest historical palaces left by the multiple dynasties that resided there. However, there are palaces that tour guides never mention and the worst part is, these palaces talk for themselves. These palaces are the Dubara Palace, The Beshtak and Al Zaafarana Palace. Looking at any of these mosques, you will definitely know to which dynasty it belongs, so take your time savoring their beauty. These mosques are not well-known to foreigners; however, locals do love them and appreciate how they survive on Cairo's land.

38. EAT LIKE A LOCAL DURING EASTER

Easter celebration in Egypt is unique, one you will never find anywhere else. In Cairo, Easter's main meal is Fesikh and Renga. This meal is basically like sushi. We eat uncooked fish. This meal is characterized by its fierce smell and taste.

Locals consider it to be a sacred habit to eat Fesikh and Renga during Easter. So, if you are visiting Cairo during spring, make sure to taste this salty original fish. Also, to live the full local experience, go buy your own Fesikh from any super market, ask for help, for sure, and make sure to order a fish that won't be too salty for your own liking. To top this and live your experience to the fullest, drink a cup of tea and add some fresh mint to it.

39. WALK IN CAIRO'S MOST BEAUTIFUL PARKS

What foreigners don't know about Cairo is that it is loaded with parks and gardens. However, as a local, I would recommend that you to visit Al Rehab city and take a walk in its parks. This compound contains more than five huge open gardens, food courts, super markets, shopping malls and even schools.

The city of Al Rehab is a destination to any local looking for natural beauty and facilities, all in one. Take a walk in the compound itself, sit in the gardens with the dogs and their friends, socialize and make new friends, and top it with a delicious meal. Restaurants there offer anything that can cross your mind, from Sushi restaurants, to Indian food restaurants.

If you are a pet lover, go to one of the Al Rehab city gardens, and take this chance to play with the purest creatures on earth.

40. BE ONE OF CAIRO'S ANIMAL ENTHUSIASTS

If you're going around Cairo like a local, then you might as well want to share the love of dogs with Cairo residents. Cairo is full of animal shelters; however, ESMA is the most active shelter. Cairo's teenagers and young adults are on a habit of constantly taking care of street dogs and cats.

To make your visit to this shelter fruitful, look up their phone number before going, ask for their operating visitor hours, what they might need that you can bring with you, and of course, ask about the shelter's location in detail. There, you can ask the supervisors to let the animals out of their houses so that you can play with them.

41. SPEND A FANCY NIGHT AT CAIRO OPERA HOUSE

A night at Cairo Opera House can never go wrong. This fancy place holds ballet shows, musical events, opera events, orchestra events, and so much more. The dress code for most events is formal or semi-formal, which allows you to have a complete fancy night.

My advice, do it like a local and attend a concert for Omar Khairat. Most Egyptians prefer to attend Omar Khairat's concert because his music is a mix of oriental, optimistic, and modern music. Wear an elegant dress or suit, and have a night you will never forget.

42. NOLA YOURSELF

Nola is a local desert bakery that serves fresh deserts on daily basis. This bakery offers a variety of cupcakes, Konafa, customized cakes, and so much more. For this place especially, I do not have any specific recommendations, eat whatever your eyes land on, every bit there is delicious and tasty. Nola Cupcakes is spread across Cairo, in approximately every district. Look it up on the internet and choose the shop that is closest to you or to where you're staying because I am sure you will go back to eat more and more of their treats.

43. DANCE AND WATCH THEM DANCE

Who doesn't love tango and salsa shows? If you're a dancer, an amateur, or even just love to watch salsa and tango dancing, then mark your calendar for two unforgettable nights. Tango nights are held every Monday at El Mojito in Conrad Hotel and Salsa nights are held on Saturdays from 9:30 to 1:30. You don't have to be an expert to go watch the dancers or even join in for a dance or two. Simply go to enjoy your time and socialize.

44. TAKE A NILE TOUR IN A FELUCCA

The Nile River and feluccas are dear friends. Any local in Cairo appreciates this friendship and even worships it. Felucca tours are our escape from our daily life and work. Take a felucca tour with locals and enjoy their spirit.

During felucca tours, locals usually play music. Try to choose a local that would grant you with Egyptian music and spirit. Together, those would definitely add up to the best experience. Also, munch up on a Meshabek bar; this desert exists only in Egypt. This felucca experience, with the music and Meshabek is an authentic local experience. Try to do this at least once.

45. GO SANDBOARDING

Egypt is blessed with vast desert spots and, lately, Egyptians decided to make peace with these spaces by sandboarding. Sandboarding is similar to snowboarding, This activity doesn't need learning. It only needs balance and a sense of adventure. Remal Adventures is my personal favourite place for sandboarding, as it organizes sandboarding inside and outside of Cairo.

Trend has it, and Cairo residents recently started adopting sandboarding as a sport of their own. Honestly, the adventure of sandboarding in Cairo gives you a feeling of belonging. Do not miss the feeling of the hot weather of Cairo, mixed with the fun and nature all at once.

46. EXPLORE AL MOEZ LI DIN ALLAH STREET

The location of this street is what enables you to roam around it for any purpose. Al Moez Street accommodates several madrassas, mosques, and palaces. The first attraction to visit in Al Moez Street is Al Madrassa of Al-Salih Ayyub, followed by Al Madrassa of Qalaun and Madrassa of Al-Nasr Mohammed. These three madrassas are the main madrassas in Al Moez street. However, they are not the only sights worth seeing.

This street is a few blocks away from Al Azhar street; make sure to pass by both streets on the same day. Also, Khan El Khalili Street is close by. Visit it to buy souvenirs, drink a cup of tea, and take pictures.

47. GO CLUBBING LIKE A LOCAL

Cairo is full of nightclubs. However, choosing one worth visiting is a hard mission. This mission is not hard because of the quality of the nightclubs, but, rather, because of the diversity of options. Each nightclub in Cairo treats its visitors with a different type of music, design, shows and events.

To enjoy clubbing in Cairo, you need to stay updated with the events that each club hosts. For me, the best choices are the nightclubs near the Nile River, or ever better, overlooking the Nile. These clubs grant you a view accompanied with good music and energetic beats.

48. PICTURES TO TAKE

Cairo is a perfect destination if you want to take perfect pictures. However, some pictures are a must in Cairo. Take a picture while climbing the Giza pyramids and a selfie at the highest point you reached. You will be proud of yourself when you see it later on! Take a picture at night in Al Moez Street, but choose a spot that has good lighting, a nice building, or a view of the market. Also, another picture that any foreigner takes in Cairo is the famous camel picture with the pyramids in the background.

Coming to modern Cairo, you can take spectacular pictures at Al Shorta Mosque in New Cairo. This modern mosque, despite being recently opened in 2017, has captured the heart of Cairo residents, with its white tiles and beautiful design. These are not the only places where you can take pictures, Cairo is full of surprises, and I'm sure you will have your mobile memory full by the time you leave Cairo.

49. VISIT COPTIC CAIRO

If you are looking to discover the Coptic history monuments filling the streets of Cairo, then Coptic Cairo is your destination. Visit the Coptic museum where you will find a collection of Coptic representative art. During your visit to this museum, you will realize how much Cairo residents love this museum. Locals like to arrange visits to this museum in order know more about the Coptic civilisation and art.

Exploring more into Coptic Cairo will lead you to the beautiful Hanging Church. This church is never empty because Cairo residents worship it, Christians and Muslims. As its name says, this church is actually hanging, and not built on the street like other buildings. Talk to the locals you meet there, you will be surprised by how much of great tour guides they can be and by how much they know each corner of this church, by heart.

Further into Coptic Cairo, Church of St. Sergius and Bacchus will grant you with its spirit. The importance of this church resides in the belief that the Holy Family, Joseph, Mary and Jesus Christ, after their journey in Egypt ended, rested in the spot where the church was built.

Finally, located near Coptic Cairo is Amr Ibn Al-As Mosque, which is the first mosque built in the city of Cairo. The architecture of this mosque is magnificent. Visit it on a Friday morning after the Friday prayer to enjoy its empty halls for yourself. The mosque, no doubt, has been restored several times; however, these restorations were a must in order to keep the oldest mosque in Cairo in shape.

50. DO THE ONE DAY TRIPS FROM CAIRO

Cairo, apart from being a city in which you will never get bored, is full of one-day-out-of-the-city activities. There are multiple one day trips that allow you to see the beauty of Egypt; however, I would recommend to do the Saint Catherine trip, the Red Sea trip, and the Fayoum trip. Each one of these trips shows you a unique type of beauty that you will never find anywhere else but in Egypt.

Saint Catherine trips are mainly held during Spring and Winter. During this trip, you go climb Mount Sinai to reach Saint Catherine. What makes this one day trip an amazing experience, is that you actually walk a long distance to reach what you want, the view from Saint Catherine. Do it towards the end of winter, maybe during May or June because it's safer to climb when the weather is not too cold. Also, do not be shy to blend in with the locals because this trip is known for being Cairo residents' favourite.

The Red Sea one-day trip has multiple choices. You can either go to Al Ain El Sokhna, which is about one hour away from Cairo, or leave at dawn and go to Al Gouna, which is about four hours away from Cairo. In both cases, you will be granted a good view, fresh air, friendly people, and beach activities. However, if you are looking for a one-day snorkeling, parasailing and diving experience, then Al Gouna is the right fit. You choose, either a day for relaxation in Al Ain El Sokhna or an adventure in Al Gouna.

Our last one-day trip is Al Fayoum. This trip is well-known among locals, and usually, tourists never even hear about it. Make sure to ask your tour guide about it. If they don't offer a program a one day trip to Al Fayoum, then ask them to link you with a company that does. During this trip you have it all, from waterfalls in the middle of nowhere, to the sandboarding activities, as well as Bedouin tea and music. Dance with the Bedouins, and learn how they dance, sip on their delicious tea, and watch the stars at night, and, of course, take pictures with them.

BONUS BOOK

50 THINGS TO KNOW ABOUT PACKING LIGHT FOR TRAVEL

PACK THE RIGHT WAY EVERY TIME

AUTHOR: MANIDIPA BHATTACHARYYA

First Published in 2015 by Dr. Lisa Rusczyk. Copyright 2015. All Rights Reserved. No part of this publication may be reproduced, including scanning and photocopying, or distributed in any form or by any means, electronic or mechanical, or stored in a database or retrieval system without prior written permission from the publisher.

Disclaimer: The publisher has put forth an effort in preparing and arranging this book. The information provided herein by the author is provided "as is". Use this information at your own risk. The publisher is not a licensed doctor. Consult your doctor before engaging in any medical activities. The publisher and author disclaim any liabilities for any loss of profit or commercial or personal damages resulting from the information contained in this book.

Edited by Melanie Howthorne

ABOUT THE AUTHOR

Manidipa Bhattacharyya is a creative writer and editor, with an education in English literature and Linguistics. After working in the IT industry for seven long years she decided to call it quits and follow her heart instead. Manidipa has been ghost writing, editing, proof reading and doing secondary research services for many story tellers and article writers for about three years. She stays in Kolkata, India with her husband and a busy two year old. In her own time Manidipa enjoys travelling, photography and writing flash fiction.

Manidipa believes in travelling light and never carries anything that she couldn't haul herself on a trip. However, travelling with her child changed the scenario. She seemed to carry the entire world with her for the baby on the first two trips. But good sense prevailed and she is again working her way to becoming a light traveler, this time with a kid.

INTRODUCTION

He who would travel happily
must travel light.

-Antoine de Saint-Exupéry

Travel takes you to different places from seas and mountains to deserts and much more. In your travels you get to interact with different people and their cultures. You will, however, enjoy the sights and interact positively with these new people even more, if you are travelling light.

When you travel light your mind can be free from worry about your belongings. You do not have to spend precious vacation time waiting for your luggage to arrive after a long flight. There is be no chance of your bags going missing and the best part is that you need not pay a fee for checked baggage.

People who have mastered this art of packing light will root for you to take only one carry-on, wherever you go. However, many people can find it really hard to pack light. More so if you are travelling with children. Differentiating between “must have” and “just in case” items is the starting point. There will be ample shopping avenues at your destination which are just waiting to be explored.

This book will show you 'packing' in a new 'light' – pun intended – and help you to embrace light packing practices for all of your future travels.

Off to packing!

DEDICATION

I dedicate this book to all the travel buffs that I know, who have given me great insights into the contents of their backpacks.

THE RIGHT TRAVEL GEAR

1. CHOOSE YOUR TRAVEL GEAR CAREFULLY

While selecting your travel gear, pick items that are light weight, durable and most importantly, easy to carry. There are cases with wheels so you can drag them along – these are usually on the heavy side because of the trolley. Alternatively a backpack that you can carry comfortably on your back, or even a duffel bag that you can carry easily by hand or sling across your body are also great options. Whatever you choose, one thing to keep in mind is that the luggage itself should not weigh a ton, this will give you the flexibility to bring along one extra pair of shoes if you so desire.

2. CARRY THE MINIMUM NUMBER OF BAGS

Selecting light weight luggage is not everything. You need to restrict the number of bags you carry as well. One carry-on size bag is ideal for light travel. Most carriers allow one cabin baggage plus one purse, handbag or camera bag as long as it slides under the seat in front. So technically, you can carry two items of luggage without checking them in.

3. PACK ONE EXTRA BAG

Always pack one extra empty bag along with your essential items. This could be a very light weight duffel bag or even a sturdy tote bag which takes up minimal space. In the event that you end up buying a lot of souvenirs, you already have a handy bag to stuff all that into and do not have to spend time hunting for an appropriate bag.

I'm very strict with my packing and have everything in its right place. I never change a rule. I hardly use anything in the hotel room. I wheel my own wardrobe in and that's it.

Charlie Watts

CLOTHES & ACCESSORIES

4. PLAN AHEAD

Figure out in advance what you plan to do on your trip. That will help you to pick that one dress you need for the occasion. If you are going to attend a wedding then you have to carry formal wear. If not, you can ditch the gown for something lighter that will be comfortable during long walks or on the beach.

5. WEAR THAT JACKET

Remember that wearing items will not add extra luggage for your air travel. So wear that bulky jacket that you plan to carry for your trip. This saves space and can also help keep you warm during the chilly flight.

6. MIX AND MATCH

Carry clothes that can be interchangeably used to reinvent your look. Find one top that goes well with a couple of pairs of pants or skirts. Use tops, shirts and jackets wisely along with other accessories like a scarf or a stole to create a new look.

7. CHOOSE YOUR FABRIC WISELY

Stuffing clothes in cramped bags definitely takes its toll which results in wrinkles. It is best to carry wrinkle free, synthetic clothes or merino tops. This will eliminate the need for that small iron you usually bring along.

8. DITCH CLOTHES PACK UNDERWEAR

Pack more underwear and socks. These are the things that will give you a fresh feel even if you do not get a chance to wear fresh clothes. Moreover these are easy to wash and can be dried inside the hotel room itself.

9. CHOOSE DARK OVER LIGHT

While picking your clothes choose dark coloured ones. They are easy to colour coordinate and can last longer before needing a wash. Accidental food spills and dirt from the road are less visible on darker clothes.

10. WEAR YOUR JEANS

Take only one pair of Jeans with you, which you should wear on the flight. Remember to pick a pair that can be worn for sightseeing trips and is equally eloquent for dinner. You can add variety by adding light weight cargoes and chinos.

11. CARRY SMART ACCESSORIES

The right accessory can give you a fresh look even with the same old dress. An intelligent neck-piece, a couple of bright scarves, stoles or a sarong can be used in a number of ways to add variety to your clothing. These light weight beauties can double up as a nursing cover, a light blanket, beach wear, a modesty cover for visiting places of worship, and also makes for an enthralling game of peek-a-boo.

12. LEARN TO FOLD YOUR GARMENTS

Seasoned travellers all swear by rolling their clothes for compact and wrinkle free packing. Bundle packing, where you roll the clothes around a central object as if tying it up, is also a popular method of compact and wrinkle free packing. Stacking folded clothes one on top of another is a big no-no as it makes creases extreme and they are difficult to get rid of without ironing.

13. WASH YOUR DIRTY LAUNDRY

One of the ways to avoid carrying loads of clothes is to wash the clothes you carry. At some places you might get to use the laundry services or a Laundromat but if you are in a pinch, best solution is to wash them yourself. If that is the plan then carrying quick drying clothes is highly recommended, which most often also happen to be the wrinkle free variety.

14. LEAVE THOSE TOWELS BEHIND

Regular towels take up a lot of space, are heavy and take ages to dry out. If you are staying at hotels they will provide you with towels anyway. If you are travelling to a remote place, where the availability of towels look doubtful, carry a light weight travel towel of viscose material to do the job.

15. USE A COMPRESSION BAG

Compression bags are getting lots of recommendation now days from regular travellers. These are useful for saving space in your luggage when you have to pack bulky dresses. While packing for the return trip, get help from the hotel staff to arrange a vacuum cleaner.

FOOTWEAR

16. PUT ON YOUR HIKING BOOTS

If you have plans to go hiking or trekking during your trip, you will need those bulky hiking boots. The best way to carry them is to wear them on flight to save space and luggage weight. You can remove the boots once inside and be comfortable in your socks.

17. PICKING THE RIGHT SHOES

Shoes are often the bulkiest items, along with being the dainty if you are a female. They need care and take up a lot of space in your luggage. It is advisable therefore to pick shoes very carefully. If you plan to do a lot of walking and site seeing, then wearing a pair of comfortable walking shoes are a must. For more formal occasions you can carry durable, light weight flats which will not take up much space.

18. STUFF SHOES

If you happen to pack a pair of shoes, ensure you utilize their hollow insides. Tuck small items like rolled up socks or belts to save space. They will also be easy to find.

TOILETRIES

19. STASHING TOILETRIES

Carry only absolute necessities. Airline rules dictate that for one carry-on bag, liquids and gels must be in 3.4 ounce (100ml) bottles or less, and must be packed in a one quart zip-lock bag. If you are planning to stay in a hotel, the basic things will be provided for you. It's best is to buy the rest from the local market at your destination.

20. TAKE ALONG TAMPONS

Tampons are a hard to find item in a lot of countries. Figure out how many you need and pack accordingly. For longer stays you can buy them online and have them delivered to where you are staying.

21. GET PAMPERED BEFORE YOU TRAVEL

Some avid travellers suggest getting a pedicure and manicure just the day before travelling. This not only gives you a well kept look, you also save the trouble of packing nail polish. Remember, every little bit of weight reduced adds up.

ELECTRONICS

22. LUGGING ALONG ELECTRONICS

Electronics have a large role to play in our lives today. Most of us cannot imagine our lives away from our phones, laptops or tablets. However while travelling, one must consider the amount of weight these electronics add to our luggage. Thankfully smart phones come along with all the essentials tools like a camera, email access, picture editing tools and more. They are smart to the point of eliminating the need to carry multiple gadgets. Choose a smart phone that suits all your requirements and travel with the world in your palms or pocket.

23. REDUCE THE NUMBER OF CHARGERS

If you do travel with multiple electronic devices, you will have to bear the additional burden of carrying all their chargers too. Check if a single charger can be used for multiple devices. You might also consider investing in a pocket charger. These small devices support multiple devices while keeping you charged on the go.

24. TRAVEL FRIENDLY APPS

Along with smart phones come numerous apps, which are immensely helpful in our travels. You name it and you have an app for it at hand – take pictures, sharing with friends and family, torch to light dark roads, maps, checking flight/train times, find hotels and many other things. Use these smart alternatives to traditional items like books to eliminate weight and save space.

I get ideas about what's essential when packing my suitcase.

-Diane von Furstenberg

TRAVELLING WITH KIDS

25. BRING ALONG THE STROLLER

Kids might enjoy walking for a while but they soon tire out and a stroller is the just the right thing for them to rest in while you continue your tour. Strollers also double duty as a luggage carrier and shopping bag holder. Remember to pick a light weight, easy to handle brand of stroller. Better yet, find out in advance if you can rent a stroller at your destination.

26. BRING ONLY ENOUGH DIAPERS FOR YOUR TRIP

Diapers take up a lot of space and add to the weight of your luggage. Therefore it is advisable to carry just enough diapers to last through the trip and a few for afterwards, till you buy fresh stock at your destination. Unless of course you are travelling to a really remote area, in which case you have no choice but to carry the load. Otherwise diapers are something you will find pretty easily.

27. TAKE ONLY A COUPLE OF TOYS

Children are easily attracted by new things in their environment. While travelling they will find numerous 'new' objects to scrutinize and play with. Packing just one favorite toy is enough, or if there is no favorite toy leave out all of them in favor of stories or imaginary games.

28. CARRY KID FRIENDLY SNACKS

Create a small snack counter in your bag to store away quick bites for those sudden hunger pangs. Depending on the child's age this could include chocolates, raisins, dry fruits, granola bars or biscuits. Also keep a bottle of water handy for your little one.

These things do not add much weight and can be adjusted in a handbag or knapsack.

29. GAMES TO CARRY

Create some travel specific, imaginary games if you have slightly grown up children, like spot the attractions. Keep a coloring book and colors handy for in-flight or hotel time. Apps on your smart phone can keep the children engaged with cartoons and story books. Older children are often entertained by games available on phones or tablets. This cuts the weight of luggage down while keeping the kids entertained.

30. LET THE KIDS CARRY THEIR LOAD

A good thing is to start early sharing of responsibilities. Let your child pick a bag of his or her choice and pack it themselves. Keep tabs on what they are stuffing in their bags by asking if they will be using that item on the trip. It could start out being just an entertainment bag initially but with growing years they will learn to sort the useful from the superfluous. Children as little as four can maneuver a small trolley suitcase like a pro- their experience in pull along toys credit. If you are worried that you may be pulling it for them, you may want to start with a backpack.

31. DECIDE ON LOCATION FOR CHILDREN TO SLEEP

While on a trip you might not always get a crib at your destination, and carrying one will make life all the more difficult. Instead call ahead to see if there are any cribs or roll out beds for children. You may even put blankets on the floor. Weave them a story about camping and they will gladly sleep without any trouble.

32. GET BABY PRODUCTS DELIVERED AT YOUR DESTINATION

If you are absolutely paranoid about not getting your favourite variety of diaper or brand of baby food, check out online stores like amazon.com for services in your destination city. You can buy things online ahead of your travel and get them delivered to your hotel upon arrival.

33. FEEDING NEEDS OF YOUR INFANTS

If you are travelling with a breastfed infant, you save the trouble of carrying bottles and bottle sanitization kits. For special food, or medications, you may need to call ahead to make sure you have a refrigerator where you are staying.

34. FEEDING NEEDS OF YOUR TODDLER

With the progression from infancy to toddler, their dietary requirements too evolve. You will have to pack some snacks for travelling time. Fresh fruits and vegetables can be purchased at your destination. Most of the cities you travel to in whichever part of the world, will have baby food products and formulas, available at the local drug-store or the supermarket.

35. PICKING CLOTHES FOR YOUR BABY

Contrary to popular belief, babies can do without many changes of clothes. At the most pack 2 outfits per day. Pack mix and match type clothes for your little one as well. Pick things which are comfortable to wear and quick to dry.

36. SELECTING SHOES FOR YOUR BABY

Like outfits, kids can make do with two pairs of comfortable shoes. If you can get some water resistant shoes it will be best. To expedite drying wet shoes, you can stuff newspaper in them then wrap them with newspaper and leave them to dry overnight.

37. KEEP ONE CHANGE OF CLOTHES HANDY

Travelling with kids can be tricky. Keep a change of clothes for the kids and mum handy in your purse or tote bag. This takes a bit of space in your hand luggage but comes extremely handy in case there are any accidents or spills.

38. LEAVE BEHIND BABY ACCESSORIES

Baby accessories like their bed, bath tub, car seat, crib etc. should be left at home. Many hotels provide a crib on request, while car seats can be borrowed from friends or rented. Babies can be given a bath in the hotel sink or even in the adult bath tub with a little bit of water. If you bring a few bath toys, they can be used in the bath, pool, and out of water. They can also be sanitized easily in the sink.

39. CARRY A SMALL LOAD OF PLASTIC BAGS

With children around there are chances of a number of soiled clothes and diapers. These plastic bags help to sort the dirt from the clean inside your big bag.

These are very light weight and come in handy to other carry stuff as well at times.

PACK WITH A PURPOSE

40. PACKING FOR BUSINESS TRIPS

One neutral-colored suit should suffice. It can be paired with different shirts, ties and accessories for different occasions. One pair of black suit pants could be worn with a matching jacket for the office or with a snazzy top for dinner.

41. PACKING FOR A CRUISE

Most cruises have formal dinners, and that formal dress usually takes up a lot of space. However you might find a tuxedo to rent. For women, a short black dress with multiple accessory options will do the trick.

42. PACKING FOR A LONG TRIP OVER DIFFERENT CLIMATES

The secret packing mantra for travel over multiple climates is layering. Layering traps air around your body creating insulation against the cold. The same light t-shirt that is comfortable in a warmer climate can be the innermost layer in a colder climate.

REDUCE SOME MORE WEIGHT

43. LEAVE PRECIOUS THINGS AT HOME

Things that you would hate to lose or get damaged leave them at home. Precious jewelry, expensive gadgets or dresses, could be anything. You will not require these on your trip. Leave them at home and spare the load on your mind.

44. SEND SOUVENIRS BY MAIL

If you have spent all your money on purchasing souvenirs, carrying them back in the same bag that you brought along would be difficult. Either pack everything in another bag and check it in the airport or get everything shipped to your home. Use an international carrier for a secure transit, but this could be more expensive than the checking fees at the airport.

45. AVOID CARRYING BOOKS

Books equal to weight. There are many reading apps which you can download on your smart phone or tab.

Plus there are gadgets like Kindle and Nook that are thinner and lighter alternatives to your regular book.

CHECK, GET, SET, CHECK AGAIN

46. STRATEGIZE BEFORE PACKING

Create a travel list and prepare all that you think you need to carry along. Keep everything on your bed or floor before packing and then think through once again – do I really need that? Any item that meets this question can be avoided. Remove whatever you don't really need and pack the rest.

47. TEST YOUR LUGGAGE

Once you have fully packed for the trip take a test trip with your luggage. Take your bags and go to town for window shopping for an hour. If you enjoy your hour long trip it is good to go, if not, go home and reduce the load some more. Repeat this test till you hit the right weight.

48. ADD A ROLL OF DUCT TAPE

You might wonder why, when this book has been talking about reducing stuff, we're suddenly asking you to pack something totally unusual. This is because when you have limited supplies, duct tape is immensely helpful for small repairs – a broken bag, leaking zip-lock bag, broken sunglasses, you name it and duct tape can fix it, temporarily.

49. LIST OF ESSENTIAL ITEMS

Even though the emphasis is on packing light, there are things which have to be carried for any trip. Here is our list of essentials:

•Passport/Visa or any other ID

•Any other paper work that might be required on a trip like permits, hotel reservation confirmations etc.

•Medicines – all your prescription medicines and emergency kit, especially if you are travelling with children

•Medical or vaccination records

•Money in foreign currency if travelling to a different country

•Tickets- Email or Message them to your phone

50. MAKE THE MOST OF YOUR TRIP

Wherever you are going, whatever you hope to do we encourage you to embrace it whole-heartedly. Take in the scenery, the culture and above all, enjoy your time away from home.

On a long journey even a straw weighs heavy.

-Spanish Proverb

PACKING AND PLANNING TIPS

A Week before Leaving

- Arrange for someone to take care of pets and water plants.
- Stop mail and newspaper.
- Notify Credit Card companies where you are going.
- Change your thermostat settings.
- Car inspected, oil is changed, and tires have the correct pressure.
- Passports and photo identification is up to date.
- Pay bills.
- Copy important items and download travel Apps.
- Start collecting small bills for tips.

Right Before Leaving

- Clean out refrigerator.
- Empty garbage cans.
- Lock windows.
- Make sure you have the proper identification with you.
- Bring cash for tips.
- Remember travel documents.
- Lock door behind you.
- Remember wallet.
- Unplug items in house and pack chargers.

>TOURIST

READ OTHER GREATER THAN A TOURIST BOOKS

Greater Than a Tourist San Miguel de Allende Guanajuato Mexico: 50 Travel Tips from a Local by Tom Peterson

Greater Than a Tourist – Lake George Area New York USA: 50 Travel Tips from a Local by Janine Hirschklau

Greater Than a Tourist – Monterey California United States: 50 Travel Tips from a Local by Katie Begley

Greater Than a Tourist – Chanai Crete Greece: 50 Travel Tips from a Local by Dimitra Papagrigoraki

Greater Than a Tourist – The Garden Route Western Cape Province South Africa: 50 Travel Tips from a Local by Li-Anne McGregor van Aardt

Greater Than a Tourist – Sevilla Andalusia Spain: 50 Travel Tips from a Local by Gabi Gazon

Greater Than a Tourist – Kota Bharu Kelantan Malaysia: 50 Travel Tips from a Local by Aditi Shukla

Children's Book: Charlie the Cavalier Travels the World by Lisa Rusczyk

>TOURIST

> TOURIST

Visit Greater Than a Tourist for Free Travel Tips
http://GreaterThanATourist.com

Sign up for the Greater Than a Tourist Newsletter for discount days, new books, and travel information:
http://eepurl.com/cxspyf

Follow us on Facebook for tips, images, and ideas:
https://www.facebook.com/GreaterThanATourist

Follow us on Pinterest for travel tips and ideas:
http://pinterest.com/GreaterThanATourist

Follow us on Instagram for beautiful travel images:
http://Instagram.com/GreaterThanATourist

> TOURIST

Please leave your honest review of this book on Amazon and Goodreads. Please send your feedback to GreaterThanaTourist@gmail.com as we continue to improve the series. We appreciate your positive and constructive feedback. Thank you.

METRIC CONVERSIONS

TEMPERATURE

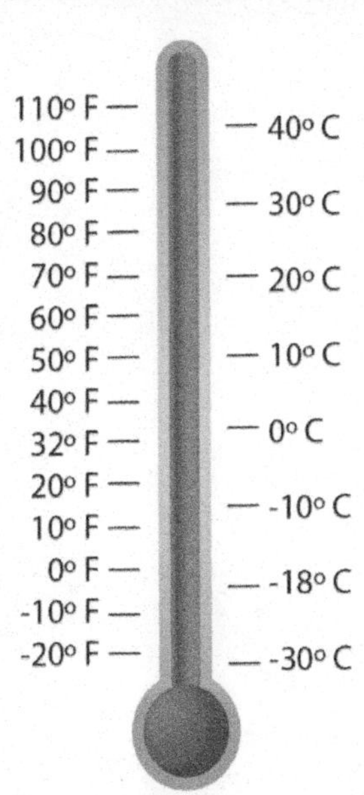

To convert F to C:

Subtract 32, and then multiply by 5/9 or .5555.

To Convert C to F:

Multiply by 1.8 and then add 32.

32F = 0C

LIQUID VOLUME

To Convert:.....................Multiply by

U.S. Gallons to Liters................. 3.8

U.S. Liters to Gallons 26

Imperial Gallons to U.S. Gallons 1.2

Imperial Gallons to Liters....... 4.55

Liters to Imperial Gallons 22

1 Liter = .26 U.S. Gallon

1 U.S. Gallon = 3.8 Liters

DISTANCE

To convert ....Multiply by

Inches to Centimeters 2.54

Centimeters to Inches 39

Feet to Meters........................ .3

Meters to Feet 3.28

Yards to Meters 91

Meters to Yards 1.09

Miles to Kilometers 1.61

Kilometers to Miles............ .62

1 Mile = 1.6 km

1 km = .62 Miles

WEIGHT

1 Ounce = .28 Grams

1 Pound = .4555 Kilograms

1 Gram = .04 Ounce

1 Kilogram = 2.2 Pounds

TRAVEL QUESTIONS

- Do you bring presents home to family or friends after a vacation?
- Do you get motion sick?
- Do you have a favorite billboard?
- Do you know what to do if there is a flat tire?
- Do you like a sun roof open?
- Do you like to eat in the car?
- Do you like to wear sun glasses in the car?
- Do you like toppings on your ice cream?
- Do you use public bathrooms?
- Did you bring your cell phone and does it have power?
- Do you have a form of identification with you?
- Have you ever been pulled over by a cop?
- Have you ever given money to a stranger on a road trip?
- Have you ever taken a road trip with animals?
- Have you ever went on a vacation alone?
- Have you ever run out of gas?

- If you could move to any place in the world, where would it be?
- If you could travel anywhere in the world, where would you travel?
- If you could travel in any vehicle, which one would it be?
- If you had three things to wish for from a magic genie, what would they be?
- If you have a driver's license, how many times did it take you to pass the test?
- What are you the most afraid of on vacation?
- What do you want to get away from the most when you are on vacation?
- What foods smells bad to you?
- What item do you bring on ever trip with you away from home?
- What makes you sleepy?
- What song would you love to hear on the radio when you're cruising on the highway?
- What travel job would you want the least?
- What will you miss most while you are away from home?
- What is something you always wanted to try?

- What is the best road side attraction that you ever saw?
- What is the farthest distance you ever biked?
- What is the farthest distance you ever walked?
- What is the weirdest thing you needed to buy while on vacation?
- What is your favorite candy?
- What is your favorite color car?
- What is your favorite family vacation?
- What is your favorite food?
- What is your favorite gas station drink or food?
- What is your favorite license plate design?
- What is your favorite restaurant?
- What is your favorite smell?
- What is your favorite song?
- What is your favorite sound that nature makes?
- What is your favorite thing to bring home from a vacation?
- What is your favorite vacation with friends?
- What is your favorite way to relax?

- Where is the farthest place you ever traveled in a car?
- Where is the farthest place you ever went North, South, East and West?
- Where is your favorite place in the world?
- Who is your favorite singer?
- Who taught you how to drive?
- Who will you miss the most while you are away?
- Who if the first person you will contact when you get to your destination?
- Who brought you on your first vacation?
- Who likes to travel the most in your life?
- Would you rather be hot or cold?
- Would you rather drive above, below, or at the speed limited?
- Would you rather drive on a highway or a back road?
- Would you rather go on a train or a boat?
- Would you rather go to the beach or the woods?

TRAVEL BUCKET LIST

1.

2.

3.

4.

5.

6.

7.

8.

9.

10.

NOTES

Made in the USA
Las Vegas, NV
29 September 2022

56186560R00069